Make Your Money Speak For You

Henry Allen

Copyright Page

Copyright Holder: © Henry Allen
Author: © Henry Allen 2025
Publisher: Univon

Release Year 2025

Index

Money as Your Most Powerful Voice

Money is much more than a medium of exchange or a tool to cover our basic needs. In the modern world, money is an extension of your personality and, in many cases, the first impression you make on others. Your financial decisions, how you spend and how you invest, speak volumes about you before you even open your mouth. When you use your money wisely, you can project an image of success, confidence and authority, no matter where you come from or what your current circumstances are.

Imagine walking into an important meeting. It's not just how you're dressed or the words you choose to introduce yourself that matter, but also what your lifestyle and choices say about you. The watch you wear, the care with which you've selected your outfit, even the level of your financial knowledge, are silent indicators of who you are and what you stand for. People notice these details, even if they don't mention them. And this is where the true power of money lies: well spent, it can open doors, command respect, and solidify your place in any environment.

The first step to making your money speak for you is to stop seeing it as something that is only earned and spent. Money is a tool that must be used strategically. When you make an expense, you must ask yourself: is this building or destroying my image? For example, spending on quality clothing is not just about luxury, but about sending a message. Each item of clothing you wear can say, “I am a person who takes care of details and values quality.” On the other hand, spending on ephemeral or unnecessary things that do not contribute to your personal goal can communicate clutter or lack of focus.

However, it's not about spending for the sake of spending. The real secret is to make every financial decision an investment in yourself. When you invest in your education, you're strengthening your ability to make smart, strategic decisions. When you choose valuable experiences, such as trips that broaden your perspective or courses that teach you in-demand skills, you're building a more valuable version of yourself. These investments not only improve your life, they also make you someone who projects confidence and knowledge.

Money also has the power to amplify your voice in the circles where it really matters. If you want to enter a world of opportunity, whether in business, society, or in a personal realm, you must understand that money gives you access. This doesn't simply mean paying for exclusive memberships or participating in fancy events, but understanding that money well spent can put you in the right place to meet the right people. A strategic meal with a mentor, a donation to an important cause, or even a thoughtful gift to someone key can be smart ways to use your resources to open doors that would otherwise remain closed.

Of course, money isn't everything. If you don't have solid principles and a clear purpose, money won't be able to do the work for you. But when your money is aligned with your values and goals, it becomes a loudspeaker for what you stand for. When you choose to spend with purpose, invest strategically, and act with vision, you're telling the world that you're a person who knows what you want and is willing to work for it. And that's one of the quickest ways to gain respect.

Often, the biggest mistake we make with money is using it as a means to impress in a superficial way. It's important to remember that it's not about appearances, but about building something real. A fancy car may attract attention, but if there's no financial stability or coherent image behind it, the effect will be counterproductive. The true impact of money is not in what you buy, but in what it represents. So, before making any major expenditure, ask yourself: does this reflect the best version of me? If the answer is yes, then you are using money as a powerful tool and not as a mere passing resource.

Money also has the ability to make you a role model. When you manage your finances responsibly and manage to build something solid with what you have, people notice. You will be seen as someone reliable, someone who knows how to handle life intelligently. This not only brings you admiration, but also opportunities. People want to work with those who inspire trust, and nothing inspires more trust than someone who uses money wisely.

The impact of money isn't just external. When you know that your finances are under control and that every expense you make has a purpose, you gain an inner confidence that carries over into everything you do. That confidence allows you to walk tall, speak clearly, and act with determination. It's a change that doesn't go unnoticed by others, and it begins when you decide to take control of your relationship with money.

In short, money is a voice that speaks for you, both when you are present and when you are not. Every financial decision you make sends a message about who you are, what you value, and where you are headed. Use your money to build, to invest in your future, to show the world your best version. No matter what your starting point is, if you decide to use your money with purpose and strategy, you will soon realize that it is your greatest ally in achieving the respect, admiration, and success you desire.

Think Like an Investor, Not a Spender

Most people view money as something to be spent. They earn it, use it to cover their needs, and the little left over goes to some treat or entertainment. This cycle repeats itself over and over again, and even if they manage to make more money, the mindset remains the same: how much can I spend with what I have. The problem with this way of thinking is that it keeps you stuck in a loop where money is always slipping away from you, no matter how much you make. If you want to build true wealth and move towards a life of financial success, you need to change this mindset completely. You need to start thinking like an investor, not a spender.

Thinking like an investor means that every time money comes into your hands, you see it as an opportunity to make that money grow, not just to use it and let it go. Investors have a simple rule: every dollar you spend should give you something in return, whether in the form of future earnings, knowledge, skills, connections, or even free time. It doesn't matter if it's a small sum or a large amount, the important thing is that every financial decision is made with the mindset of earning a return, something that propels you forward rather than just satisfying a momentary desire.

An easy way to start thinking like an investor is to question yourself every time you spend money. Ask yourself: Is this an expense or an investment? For example, buying trendy clothes that will be out of style in a few months may be an unnecessary expense. But investing in good quality, classic-style clothing that will last for years can be a smart investment, as it will project an image of trust and professionalism. The difference is in the purpose behind the decision. An expense gives you something ephemeral; an investment gives you something lasting.

Another key to adopting this mindset is to understand the concept of the value of money over time. Every dollar you have today has the potential to multiply if you invest it correctly. Instead of spending that money on something that will lose value or disappear, you could use it to buy an asset that makes more money, such as a mutual fund, stocks, real estate, or even a business idea. An investor always thinks in terms of growth: how they can turn what they have today into something much bigger tomorrow.

But it's not just about investing in financial markets or material goods. You should also think about investing in yourself. Spending money on a course that improves your skills, on books that expand your knowledge, or on experiences that give you a new perspective is one of the most valuable investments you can make. What you learn and the connections you make through these investments can open doors you never even imagined. Every penny you invest in your personal and professional development is a step toward a better version of yourself, one that is more capable of generating income and taking advantage of opportunities.

Of course, thinking like an investor also involves learning to say no. No to impulse purchases, no to unnecessary spending, no to temptations that don’t bring you anything of value. This doesn’t mean you have to deprive yourself of everything. It means you have to be selective and mindful of where you put your money. You’re not saying no because you can't spend, but because you're choosing to use your money in a way that will benefit you in the long run. That's the difference between someone who spends and someone who invests.

An investor also understands the importance of patience. Invested money doesn't always yield immediate results, and that's okay. Financial growth is a process that takes time, and the best investments are often those that require consistency and a long-term view. This means you must be willing to sacrifice immediate gratifications in order to reap much greater rewards in the future. For example, instead of spending your money on an expensive dinner every weekend, you could invest that amount into a savings fund or a project that generates additional income.

Furthermore, investors are informed people. They don't blindly make financial decisions or follow fads without understanding them. If you're thinking about investing, whether in a business, real estate, or any other asset, it's essential that you take the time to learn. Read, ask questions, research, and make sure you understand what you're putting your money into. Financial education isn't optional if you want to think like an investor; it's a critical part of your success.

Adopting this mindset will not only help you build wealth, but it will also give you a sense of control over your financial life. You will stop feeling like money rules you and start seeing it as a tool that you control. Every dollar you invest, rather than spend, will bring you one step closer to your goals and dreams. This way of thinking will also influence how others view you. When people notice that you manage your money intelligently and purposefully, they respect you more and perceive you as someone trustworthy and visionary.

Ultimately, thinking like an investor means you're building a future for yourself and those around you. Every financial decision you make, no matter how small, can make the difference between staying where you are or moving toward a life of freedom and unlimited possibilities. Shifting your mindset may feel like a small adjustment at first, but over time, you'll find that it's one of the most powerful changes you can make to transform your life. Your money has the potential to be so much more than a means to pay bills. It can be the engine that drives your success—as long as you choose to use it strategically and with a clear vision.

The Psychology of Financial Respect

Financial respect is not just about how much money you have, but how you manage it, use it, and project it to the world. We live in a society where people look more than they say, and while respect should not depend on material things, in practice, your financial decisions play a crucial role in how others perceive you. The psychology of financial respect is based on clear principles: stability, trust, vision, and consistency. These elements build a reputation that attracts admiration and opportunities.

One of the most important factors in generating financial respect is stability. It doesn't matter if you have a modest income or a considerable fortune; if people perceive that you manage your finances in an orderly and responsible manner, you will automatically earn their respect. Financial stability doesn't mean being a millionaire, but rather showing that you live within your means, that you don't get carried away by impulses, and that you always have a plan. Someone who is always in debt, taking out loans to cover basic expenses, or spending in an uncontrolled manner, projects an image of disorganization, which erodes the respect that others might have for them.

Confidence is also key. When people see that you handle your money confidently, make thoughtful financial decisions, and aren't afraid to invest in yourself or your goals, they perceive you as someone in control of your life. Financial confidence doesn't mean you never make mistakes, but rather that you learn from them and move forward with a more solid strategy. When you project this confidence, you inspire others to trust you, whether it's to do business with you, ask you for advice, or even follow you as a leader.

Another key aspect of financial respect is vision. People respect those who are clear about where they are going and how they plan to get there. If you have clear financial goals and are constantly working towards them, it shows. You may not have everything you want right now, but if others see that you are building something, that you are investing time and resources into your future, they will respect you for your focus and determination. Having vision also means avoiding comparing yourself to others and staying true to your own goals. Respect doesn’t come from pretending to be something you are not, but from being authentic and consistent with your path.

Consistency is the common thread that ties everything together. If your financial actions don't reflect your values or goals, people will sense a disconnect. For example, someone who constantly talks about saving, but impulsively spends on unnecessary things, loses credibility. Consistency also applies to how you treat others with your money. Being generous, without being excessive, and helping those in need in a sensible way reinforces your image as someone worthy of respect. Conversely, using money to show off or humiliate others can lead to rejection, not admiration.

A common mistake many people make is trying to buy financial respect through material possessions. While a fancy car, a fancy house, or designer clothing may impress momentarily, true financial respect is not based on what you have, but on how you got it and how you handle it. People may admire your possessions, but they will respect more your ability to maintain them, your work ethic, and your discipline. Material things may get the attention, but your financial principles are what leave a lasting impression.

The psychology of financial respect also has to do with how you deal with financial challenges. We all face difficulties at some point, but the way you handle them says a lot about who you are. If you are seen facing financial problems calmly, looking for smart solutions and not letting stress consume you, that generates admiration. On the other hand, if you react with desperation or neglect your responsibilities, you may lose the respect of those around you.

It's also important to understand that financial respect is not something that is demanded, but rather earned. This means that you need to be patient and consistent in your actions. Don't expect people to recognize your achievements right away, but be assured that over time, your discipline and decisions will speak for themselves. Financial respect is a reflection of your character, and building it takes dedication.

Finally, financial respect not only has an external impact, but also an internal one. When you know that you manage your money intelligently and with purpose, you feel more confident about yourself. That confidence is projected into how you communicate, how you make decisions, and how you face challenges. It's a positive cycle: the better you manage your finances, the more confident you are, and the more confident you are, the more respect you generate. This respect, in turn, opens doors, creates opportunities, and positions you as someone worthy of admiration.

The psychology of financial respect is not based on tricks or displaying false status. It is based on solid principles and conscious decisions. If you want to be respected for how you manage your money, start by establishing a solid financial foundation, being consistent with your values, and always acting with vision and purpose. Financial respect is not just a result, but a powerful tool that can transform your life and the way you relate to others. With every decision you make, you will be building not only your financial future, but also a reputation that will be hard to ignore.

The Art of Financial Elegance

Financial elegance is not about how much money you have, but how you use it and make it work for you. It is the ability to project confidence, control and sophistication in your financial decisions. You don't have to be a millionaire to be elegant with your finances; what matters is the mindset behind your choices and the way you build your life around them. Financial elegance is discreet, strategic and always with a clear purpose.

For starters, financial elegance means living below your means, but with style. This doesn't mean depriving yourself of things you love or living in extreme austerity, but rather learning to distinguish between what really has value and what is just an unnecessary expense. For example, instead of buying cheap clothes that you'll have to constantly replace, invest in quality garments that will not only last longer, but will also make you look impeccable. It's not about the quantity, but the quality of your choices.

Financial elegance is also reflected in your ability to plan. Financially elegant people don't act on impulse. Before they spend, they think about how that decision will impact their long-term well-being. If you decide to go on vacation, instead of charging it all to a credit card and paying months of interest, plan ahead, save, and pay cash. Not only does this free you from the stress of debt, but it shows that you know how to manage your resources responsibly.

Another key aspect of financial class is discretion. You don't need to announce to the world every purchase you make or how much money you make. Truly classy people don't seek validation through their wealth. Instead, they let their actions speak for themselves. A well-managed lifestyle and a confident attitude say much more than any social media post showing off unnecessary luxuries. True class is in the peace of mind that comes from knowing you have your finances under control.

Investing strategically is another pillar of financial smartness. Instead of spending on things that lose value quickly, like luxury cars or unnecessary gadgets, direct your money toward assets that generate income or increase in value over time. Buying property, investing in your education, or even starting your own business are all decisions that reflect a mindset focused on growth and stability. These investments not only improve your financial situation, but they also project an image of someone who has clear goals and is working to achieve them.

The art of financial grace also includes taking care of your relationships. The way you treat people with your money says a lot about you. Being generous when appropriate, paying on time, and avoiding unnecessary arguments over financial matters all reflect maturity and thoughtfulness. You don't need to be extravagant to be generous; sometimes a small gesture, such as inviting someone out for coffee or helping a friend in need, can speak more about your character than any luxury.

Additionally, financial elegance involves having an emergency fund. This is one of the clearest ways to demonstrate that you have control over your finances. When you have enough savings to handle unexpected events without panicking or going into debt, you project an image of stability and foresight. Knowing that you are prepared for the unexpected not only gives you peace of mind, but also allows you to face any situation with confidence.

Time management also plays a role in financial elegance. Valuing your time means not wasting it on activities that do not add value to your life or contribute to your personal and financial growth. For example, instead of spending hours searching for meaningless discounts, you could use that time to learn something new or develop a skill that increases your earning capacity. Elegance is not in extreme frugality, but in the efficiency of your decisions.

A common mistake is to confuse financial elegance with luxury. While luxury can be a part of your life, it should not define it. Financial elegance is more about balance than extravagance. You can enjoy nice things and exclusive experiences, but always within your means and with a clear purpose. Senseless luxury tends to impress in the short term, while elegant decisions build a lasting legacy.

Finally, financial smartness includes having a continuous learning mindset. Financially smart people are always looking for ways to improve their relationship with money. They read about finances, take courses, seek advice, and aren't afraid to ask questions. They understand that knowledge is one of the most powerful tools to build a balanced and fulfilling life.

In conclusion, financial elegance is not something you buy, but something you build through smart, consistent, and strategic decisions. It is the ability to live with purpose, enjoy what you have, and project an image of confidence and control. By adopting this mindset, you will not only improve your financial situation, but you will also gain the respect and admiration of those around you. Because in the end, true elegance is not in how much you have, but in how you manage it.

Strategic Investments in Your Personal Brand

Investing in your personal brand is one of the smartest and most profitable decisions you can make. Your personal brand is the perception that others have of you, and that perception has a direct impact on the opportunities that are presented to you, how people value you, and the level of trust you inspire. A strong personal brand can open doors that would otherwise remain closed. That's why every peso you invest in building, improving, and projecting your personal brand is a step toward a more successful future.

The first step in investing in your personal brand is to identify what you want others to see in you. What values do you want to convey? What kind of professional or person do you want people to remember you as? Defining this is crucial because it will be the basis for all your investments. For example, if you want to be perceived as someone innovative, you will need to invest in tools, knowledge, and skills that reinforce that image. If you want to be seen as trustworthy and professional, you will need to make sure that every aspect of your presence, from the way you dress to the way you communicate, reflects those qualities.

An essential investment for your personal brand is your education and professional development. No matter what stage of life you are in, there is always something new to learn. This can be a specialized course in your area, a diploma in soft skills such as leadership or communication, or even learning an additional language. These investments not only improve your capabilities, but also position you as someone who cares about growing and staying up to date. People value those who are constantly evolving and adding more value.

In addition to education, image is a crucial component of your personal brand. This isn't about being superficial, but about understanding that we live in a world where first impressions count. Investing in the right clothes, a good haircut, or even a professional photo shoot can make a huge difference in how others perceive you. You don't need to spend a fortune, but you do need to make sure your appearance is consistent with the image you want to project. If you want to be seen as a trusted leader, dress like one. If you aspire to a creative role, reflect that creativity in your style.

Another important aspect is your digital presence. In today's age, the way you present yourself online can be just as important as your physical presence. Invest in creating and maintaining professional profiles on social media like LinkedIn, where you can showcase your accomplishments, share relevant content, and connect with people in your industry. Also consider having a personal website or online portfolio that highlights your skills, projects, and values. This is an investment that will not only give you visibility, but will also allow you to control the narrative about who you are and what you stand for.

Communication is another pillar of your personal brand that deserves investment. Knowing how to express your ideas clearly, confidently, and persuasively is a skill that can set you apart from the rest. You can invest in public speaking workshops, professional writing training, or even a communication coach. The way you speak and write says a lot about you, and people tend to respect and follow those who know how to convey their ideas effectively.

Networking is also a critical part of building your personal brand. Here, investing means not just attending events, but also being willing to spend time and money building meaningful relationships. This can include attending conferences, joining professional associations, attending workshops, or even inviting key people in your industry to coffee to learn from them. These connections will not only help you expand your network of contacts, but will also reinforce your reputation as someone who is interested and engaged.

Finally, don't underestimate the power of investing in experiences. Experiences enrich your life and add depth to your personal brand. Traveling, volunteering, or getting involved in projects you're passionate about not only broaden your perspective, but they also make you more interesting and authentic to others. People admire those who have stories to tell and lessons to share. Every experience you live becomes a unique element that strengthens your identity.

Investing in your personal brand is an ongoing process. It's not something you do once and forget, but rather a continuous effort to improve and adapt. With every investment you make, whether in your education, your image, your connections, or your experiences, you're building a legacy that will represent you in every room you walk into, even those where you're not physically present.

In the end, your personal brand is what people say about you when you're not in the room. Investing in it will not only impact your professional success, but also the way others respect and value you. Every effort you make to strengthen it is an investment in yourself, your future, and the endless possibilities that will open up before you.

The Visual Impact of Success

The visual impact of success is one of the most powerful and underrated tools for conveying confidence, authority, and professionalism. We live in a world where first impressions count, and while many people insist that we shouldn't judge others by their appearance, the reality is that we do, almost instinctively. Your physical presence and how you choose to present yourself to the world can open or close doors before you even utter a single word. Success has a look, and learning to strategically project it can change the way others perceive you.

The first step to making a visual impact is to understand that your appearance not only reflects your personality, but also your values, ambitions, and level of preparation. Dressing well doesn't mean spending large sums of money on designer clothes, but rather investing in quality pieces that are consistent with the message you want to convey. A well-fitting suit, clean shoes, and a well-groomed style project professionalism and attention to detail. If you work in a more casual environment, you can achieve the same by choosing clothes that are modern, clean, and appropriate for the occasion.

Every time you show up, you're sending a message, and that message needs to be clear and congruent with your goals.

Your personal hygiene is equally crucial. Well-groomed hair, clean nails, and a pleasant scent are small but essential details. These things not only reflect respect for yourself, but also for the people you interact with. Taking care of your physical appearance is not an act of vanity, but a way to show that you take yourself and others seriously. When you project a well-groomed image, people automatically see you as someone trustworthy and organized.

The visual impact of success also extends to the objects around you. This includes everything from the design of your workspace to the tools you use on a daily basis. A tidy, well-decorated office speaks of efficiency and good taste. A clean, well-maintained car conveys responsibility and pride in what you have, regardless of its price. Even something as simple as the notebook you take notes in or the design of your business card can influence how others perceive you. These details communicate who you are and how much you care about the impression you leave.

Posture and body language also play a vital role in the visual impact of success. An upright posture, walking confidently, and maintaining eye contact demonstrate confidence and determination. Successful people not only look good, but they also move in ways that project control and leadership. Avoid nervous gestures, such as fidgeting with your hands or avoiding the gaze of others, as these can weaken the confident image you are trying to project.

Another key element is consistency between your appearance and your message. If you say you are an expert in your field, but present yourself in a sloppy manner, people will have a hard time trusting you. Consistency creates credibility, and credibility is essential for success. This doesn't mean you need to change who you are, but you need to align your appearance with your goals and the context in which you operate. If you are in a creative industry, you can afford to be more expressive with your style, but if you work in a corporate environment, it's best to opt for a more formal and conservative approach.

The visual impact of success is not limited to what you wear, but also includes how you interact with the digital environment. Your social media profiles, your profile picture, and the quality of your posts are all part of your visual presence. A well-designed profile and professional photos convey seriousness and commitment to your image. Remember that, in many cases, people will first get to know you online before meeting you in person, so investing in a quality digital presence is just as important as taking care of your physical image.

Success is also about how you handle your money in terms of visual impact. It's not about showing off, but about using your money wisely to build a positive perception. For example, investing in a nice watch, a quality handbag, or a stylish pair of shoes can be a subtle but powerful sign of your attention to detail and appreciation for quality. These items don't need to be extravagant or expensive; they simply need to be representative of someone who values what they own and uses it with purpose.

It is important to note that the visual impact of success should not be superficial. It is not about building an empty facade, but about using your appearance to reinforce what you already are and what you are working to achieve. Success starts from within, with your skills, values and attitude, but the visual impact helps those qualities to be noticed and recognized by others. It is a tool that complements your efforts and enhances them.

Finally, remember that projecting visual success doesn't mean you have to impress everyone. What matters is that your image is authentic and reflects the best of yourself. At the end of the day, the visual impact of success is not about pleasing others, but about building a presence that supports you, gives you confidence, and helps you open doors to your goals. When people see you as successful, they are more inclined to trust you, listen to you, and offer you opportunities. Harness the power of perception and use it as a tool to advance on your path to success.

Make Your Money Work Harder Than You Do

The real power of money is not in spending it, but in making it work for you. Most people spend their entire lives working to earn money, but truly successful people understand that money should be a tool, not the end goal. When you make your money work harder than you, you create a system where your income is not solely dependent on your time or effort. This not only allows you to earn more, but also enjoy greater freedom and stability in your life.

To make your money work harder than you do, you first need to change your mindset. Stop seeing money as something that just comes in and out of your bank account every month. Start seeing it as a resource that can grow if you manage it correctly. Imagine that every penny you have is like an employee that can generate more income if you put it in the right place. But, just like an employee needs direction and purpose, your money also needs a strategy to multiply.

The first step is to save, but not just any old way. Saving without a clear purpose is like storing water in a bucket with leaks: it eventually goes to waste. Set up an emergency fund that covers at least three to six months of your basic expenses. This fund is not an investment; it's your safety net for unexpected events. Once you have it, any extra money you save should be earmarked for making more money, not sitting idle in a bank account. Money stored in cash loses value over time due to inflation, so your goal should be to put it to work as soon as possible.

Investing is the key to making your money work for you. Smart investments allow you to grow your money without having to constantly work for it. There are many options, and choosing the right one depends on your goals, your risk tolerance, and how long you are willing to wait to see results. For example, you can invest in stocks or index funds that allow you to earn returns over the long term. You can also consider real estate, where a rental property can provide you with steady passive income. Even owning a business, when strategically managed, is a powerful way to grow your money.

A fundamental aspect of investing is understanding the power of compound interest. This principle is the foundation of many financial growth strategies. Essentially, compound interest means that your earnings generate more earnings over time. For example, if you invest in a fund that gives you a ten percent return per year, you not only earn money on your initial investment, but also on the earnings you made in the previous year. Over time, this effect can be huge. Compound interest is not immediate, but the sooner you start, the more powerful it will be.

Diversifying your investments is another important point. Never put all your money in one place. Diversification reduces risk and increases the chances of success. If one investment doesn't work out as you expected, others can make up for the losses. For example, you could have part of your money in the stock market, another in real estate, and another in a savings fund with fixed returns. In this way, you create a balanced portfolio that minimizes risks and maximizes opportunities.

Aside from investing, another way to make your money work for you is to create passive income streams. These are income streams that don't require your constant intervention. For example, writing a book, developing an online course, or patenting a product can generate income for you for years after you've done the initial work. You can also earn passive income through stock dividends or rental income from properties. The more passive income streams you have, the less you'll be dependent on your time to make money.

Automation is also a powerful tool to make your money work harder than you do. Set up automatic transfers that deposit a portion of your income into investment or savings accounts. This eliminates the temptation to spend money and ensures that you are always growing your capital. Also, take advantage of available technologies, such as financial apps, to monitor and manage your investments without dedicating hours of your time each week.

It is important to mention that knowledge is an investment in itself. Before you put your money anywhere, make sure you understand what you are doing. You don't need to be an expert, but you do need to be informed. Read books, take courses, and consult with financial advisors if necessary. Every penny you invest in your financial education has the potential to multiply many times over throughout your life.

Finally, remember that making your money work for you requires patience and consistency. It's not about getting rich overnight, but rather building a system that grows steadily over time. There will be times when the results aren't immediate, but if you continue to invest strategically and control your spending, you'll eventually reach a point where the money you make from your investments will outweigh the money you make from your work.

Making your money work harder than you do isn't just a financial strategy, it's a way of life. It's about learning to prioritize the future over the present, making smart decisions, and making the most of the resources you have. When you do this, you not only improve your financial situation, but you also gain freedom, time, and peace of mind. That's what it really means to own your money instead of it owning you.

The Golden Net

The golden network is the set of connections you build throughout your life, and if managed correctly, it can become one of the most valuable assets you possess. This network is not made of physical threads, but of relationships, trust, and opportunities. It is a powerful tool that can help you achieve your goals, open unexpected doors, and multiply your influence in ways you can't even imagine. Building and maintaining this network is not something that happens overnight; it requires time, effort, and a strategic approach.

The first step to building your golden network is to understand that every person has something valuable to offer, whether it's an idea, a contact, a resource, or just a different perspective. Never underestimate the power of a conversation with someone new. Often, the biggest opportunities don't come directly from the people closest to you, but from indirect connections. That's why it's critical to keep an open mind and be willing to interact with people outside of your usual circle. The key here is quality over quantity. It's not about meeting everyone, but about building meaningful relationships with people who share your values and goals or who can complement them.

Investing in your golden network means giving before receiving. Genuine relationships are not built on what you can get, but on what you can contribute. Help others whenever you can, whether it's sharing advice, connecting them with someone they know, or simply listening to their problems. This approach builds trust and reciprocity. When people see that you're willing to help without expecting anything in return, they'll be more inclined to return the favor when you need it.

To build a strong network, you also need to be proactive. Attend events, conferences, and workshops related to your industry or personal interests. These are perfect opportunities to meet people who share your passions and goals. Don't be afraid to start conversations. A simple question, like what brought them to the event or what they're passionate about about their job, can be the start of a valuable connection. Make sure you bring business cards with you, or at least be prepared to exchange contact information in a professional manner.

Once you start building your network, the key is to maintain it. A network that isn't nurtured eventually weakens. This means that you need to be in regular contact with the people in your circle. It doesn't have to be complicated. An occasional message, a call to catch up, or even a comment on their social media posts can be enough to keep the relationship going. The important thing is that people feel that you are genuinely interested in them, not just when they need something.

The power of a well-built golden network lies in its ability to amplify your resources and skills. For example, imagine you are looking for funding for a project. If you have a strong network, you might be able to find someone who is willing to invest in you or connect you with someone who is. Similarly, if you need advice in a specific area, chances are someone in your network has the necessary expertise or knows someone who can help you. These are the advantages of having a network: you don't have to know everything or do everything on your own.

Technology is an invaluable tool for building and managing your golden network. Social media platforms like LinkedIn are platforms specifically designed for making professional connections. Use them to share relevant content, interact with your contacts, and stay up to date on what's happening in your industry. Don't limit yourself to the digital realm, though. Face-to-face connections are still the strongest and most memorable. Whenever possible, look for opportunities to interact in person.

It's important to mention that a golden network is not only about what others can do for you, but also what you can do for them. Often times, the greatest opportunities come from acting as a bridge between two people who could mutually benefit. Becoming a connector within your network not only increases your value to others, but also strengthens the relationships between the people in your circle.

Finally, never forget the importance of authenticity in building your network. People can easily spot when someone isn't genuine. Be honest about your intentions and make sure your actions reflect your words. Building a golden network isn't a short-term project, it's a long-term investment that requires integrity and commitment. Authenticity is what makes relationships lasting and valuable.

In short, your golden network is not just a group of contacts, it is an ecosystem of relationships that can significantly influence your personal and professional success. To build it, you must be intentional, generous, and consistent. Nurture these connections with care and attention, and you will find that this network not only provides you with opportunities, but also support, inspiration, and resources that outweigh any monetary value. At the end of the day, your golden network is one of the most important assets you can have, and its true value is measured in the opportunities and doors it opens in your life.

Gaining Respectability Through Social Impact

Social impact is not only a way to give something positive back to the world, but also a powerful strategy to gain respectability and build a strong reputation. We live in an era where people value those who use their resources not only for personal gain, but also to make a difference in society. Gaining respectability through social impact is not about making occasional or superficial donations, but about authentically committing to causes that reflect your values and vision.

The first step to making a social impact is to identify the areas in which you want to make a difference. These areas should resonate with you personally. This could be education, the environment, social equality, health, or any other cause that you feel close to. When you get involved in a cause that you truly care about, it's easier to dedicate time, resources, and effort, and your commitment is perceived as genuine. Authenticity is key, because people not only value what you do, but also why you do it.

Once you've identified your cause, you need to define how you'll contribute. This can involve a combination of time, money, and skills. For example, if education is important to you, you could fund scholarships for underprivileged students, donate school supplies to under-resourced schools, or even give inspirational talks to young people. If you care about the environment, you could invest in reforestation projects, support organizations that promote sustainability, or start awareness campaigns. The key is to find a way to contribute that is not only meaningful, but also sustainable over time.

Effective social impact requires planning and consistency. It's not about a one-time act, but rather an ongoing commitment. By getting involved over the long term, you not only create deeper change, but you also show that you take your role as a changemaker seriously. For example, if you decide to support a charity, do so on a regular basis, whether through recurring donations, volunteering, or active participation in their projects. This type of commitment not only benefits the cause, but also builds a perception of you as someone trustworthy and dedicated.

In addition to contributing directly, you can also multiply your impact by inspiring others to join in. Share your initiatives and experiences in your personal and professional circles. This doesn't mean bragging, but rather showing how people can make a difference and encouraging them to do the same. For example, if you're organizing a fundraising campaign, you could invite your colleagues, friends, and family to participate. In this way, you not only expand the reach of your impact, but you also position yourself as a leader who motivates and guides others toward change.

Social impact can also be integrated into your professional activities. If you are a business owner or entrepreneur, consider how your business can contribute to the well-being of the community. This could include implementing sustainable practices, donating a percentage of your profits to a cause, offering employment to people in vulnerable situations, or partnering with non-profit organizations. These actions not only benefit society, but also increase the positive perception of your company and, by extension, of you as a leader.

It's important to mention that social impact doesn't always require large amounts of money. Often, your time, experience, and skills can be even more valuable. For example, if you're a lawyer, you could offer free advice to people who can't afford it. If you're a doctor, you could get involved in health campaigns in underprivileged communities. If you're knowledgeable in a specific area, you could offer mentoring to young people interested in learning. These acts of generosity not only help others, but they also strengthen your reputation as someone committed and altruistic.

Another powerful way to create social impact is through strategic partnerships. Working with other individuals, companies, or organizations with similar goals amplifies your ability to create change. For example, if you decide to fund a youth training program, you could partner with an educational institution to ensure the program has a broader reach and better results. Partnerships not only increase the effectiveness of your efforts, but they also position you as someone who knows how to work as a team and build bridges to achieve common goals.

Social impact also has a ripple effect on your personal and professional life. By getting involved in these initiatives, you expand your network of contacts and strengthen your relationships. Many times, you will meet like-minded people who can become allies, partners, or even friends. In addition, these actions give you a sense of purpose and satisfaction that cannot be measured in financial terms alone. Knowing that you are contributing to something bigger than yourself fills you with pride and motivates you to keep going.

Finally, it's critical to be transparent in your social impact efforts. Make sure your actions are visible and verifiable, especially if they involve other people or significant resources. Share results and progress honestly, showing both achievements and challenges. Transparency builds trust and shows that you are genuinely committed to the cause.

Gaining respectability through social impact is not just a strategy, it is a way of life. It is a statement of your values and what you stand for as a person. It is a way to demonstrate that success is not only measured by what you accumulate, but also by what you give. When you act with a purpose beyond your own interests, people see you as someone worthy of respect and admiration. Ultimately, social impact not only transforms the world around you, but it also transforms you, making you stronger, wiser, and more respected.

The Power of Exclusivity

Exclusivity is a concept that appeals because it represents something that not everyone can have. It is that element that separates the ordinary from the extraordinary, the common from the exceptional. In a world where many things are within everyone's reach, exclusivity has immense power. It is a silent message that says: this is special, valuable and reserved only for a few. But exclusivity is not only about luxury items or unattainable experiences, but about how you create a sense of unique value around yourself, your actions and your choices.

The power of exclusivity lies in its ability to attract attention, respect, and admiration. When something is exclusive, people want it more. This doesn't just apply to luxury products like watches, cars, or property, but also to your time, skills, and the opportunities you offer. If everything you have or do is always available to everyone, it loses its perceived value. Conversely, when something is limited or difficult to obtain, it is automatically perceived as more desirable.

The first step to harnessing the power of exclusivity is to understand that it's not just about appearances, but about building true value behind what you offer. For example, if you're a professional, make sure your work is exceptional and difficult to replicate. This can be achieved through experience, specialized knowledge, or a unique skill. When people recognize that what you do is different and high-quality, they'll be willing to pay more or go the extra mile to work with you. Exclusivity isn't just a marketing gimmick; it's the result of being great at what you do.

In the professional world, you can use exclusivity to position yourself as unique. This starts with how you manage your time. If you are available to everyone all the time, people won't value your attention. Learn to say no strategically. When you carefully select who you dedicate your time and efforts to, people start to value you more. This doesn't mean being inaccessible for no reason, but rather showing that you value your time enough to only spend it on what really matters.

Exclusivity can also be reflected in your choices. For example, instead of attending every social or business event, select those that truly align with your goals and values. By doing so, you not only protect your time, but you also reinforce the perception that you are someone who carefully chooses where to be and who to associate with. People respect those who are selective because it sends a clear message: you know your worth and you don't settle for less.

In material terms, exclusivity isn't always about price, but about the story and meaning behind the things you own. For example, a custom garment or a unique piece of art has a much higher value than something mass-produced, not because it's expensive, but because it tells a story and represents something special. If you decide to invest in material goods to project exclusivity, do so wisely. Look for pieces that truly reflect your style and personality, rather than following trends that will disappear in a few months.

Another way to use exclusivity to your advantage is to create unique experiences for the people around you. This can apply to both your personal and professional life. For example, if you're hosting an event or meeting, make it feel special. Pay attention to the details, carefully select your guests, and make sure it's memorable. It doesn't have to be extravagant or expensive, but it should reflect a level of care and attention that people don't find elsewhere. When you create these types of experiences, people not only remember them, but they also associate you with something unique and special.

The power of exclusivity can also apply to how you present your ideas and projects. If you have a proposition that you truly believe is valuable, don’t try to sell it to everyone. Instead, identify the people or groups who would benefit most from it and present it as something created specifically for them. This approach not only increases interest, but also raises the perceived value of what you’re offering. People want to feel special, and when you give them something that feels tailor-made for them, they value it more.

Exclusivity isn’t just an external strategy; it’s also a mindset you need to adopt. It means knowing that you don’t have to say yes to everything or try to please everyone. It means understanding that your value isn't based on how many people want something from you, but on the quality of the relationships and opportunities you build. When you learn to value your time, skills, and resources, you begin to project an image of someone who knows their worth and isn't afraid to protect it.

It's important to note that exclusivity should not be confused with arrogance or elitism. It's not about looking down on others or acting like you're superior. It's about understanding your value and making sure that what you offer is perceived as meaningful and special. True exclusivity doesn't exclude, but rather elevates. It inspires others to aspire to something better and shows that it's possible to create something unique when you're committed to it.

Finally, remember that exclusivity is not a goal in itself, but a tool to strengthen your position, generate respect, and differentiate yourself in a world full of options. When you learn to harness its power intelligently, you not only increase your value to others, but you also become someone who inspires and leaves a lasting impression. Exclusivity is, at its core, the art of being unique and making others recognize it.

The Intelligence of Luxury

Luxury is a concept that many people associate with excess, opulence and ostentation. However, in its most intelligent form, luxury is not simply spending for the sake of spending, but strategically investing in things that elevate your quality of life, strengthen your image and contribute to your social and professional standing. Luxury intelligence consists of understanding when, where and how to use it to maximize its impact, without falling into superficiality or financial recklessness.

Smart luxury isn't about accumulating expensive things, but rather about carefully selecting items that truly add value to your life. It's about understanding that not everything that is expensive is valuable, and not everything that is valuable has to be expensive. For example, instead of impulsively spending on trendy products that will go out of style in a few months, you can invest in classic, well-designed, high-quality pieces that will not only make you look better, but will also stand the test of time. This applies to clothing as well as accessories, furniture, art, or any other item that is part of your lifestyle.

One of the pillars of smart luxury is quality. Instead of buying in bulk, focus on acquiring fewer things, but of better quality. Not only does this allow you to enjoy superior objects and experiences, but it also projects an image of someone who values what they own. For example, one business meeting at an exclusive restaurant can have a much bigger impact than ten meetings at generic places. It's not the act of spending that matters, but how you do it and what message it conveys.

Luxury intelligence also involves knowing when to use it to strengthen your reputation and generate valuable connections. For example, if you have the opportunity to attend a high-profile event, investing in good attire, suitable transportation, and an impeccable presentation can open doors that would otherwise remain closed. Luxury, when used strategically, not only impresses, but also creates a perception of success and authority that can be decisive in social and professional settings.

However, luxury doesn't always have to be visible to others. Often, the most valuable luxury is the one you enjoy in private, such as a vacation to an exclusive place that allows you to disconnect from stress, a personalized service that saves you time, or an investment in your physical and mental well-being. These luxuries are not necessarily for show, but they have a profound impact on your quality of life and your ability to perform at your best in your daily activities. Luxury intelligence includes knowing how to balance between what you show the world and what you do for yourself.

Another important aspect of smart luxury is authenticity. Don't try to imitate other people's consumption habits just for show. The most powerful luxury is the kind that is aligned with your values, interests, and personal style. For example, if you enjoy art, investing in original pieces that resonate with you can be much more meaningful than spending on something simply because it's trendy. When you choose luxury authentically, you project confidence and originality, which in turn strengthens your image and reputation.

Luxury intelligence also extends to how you manage your finances. It's a common misconception that luxury always involves spending large sums of money. In reality, smart luxury is often about making strategic choices that maximize the value of what you purchase. This could include waiting for the right time to buy, doing research to find high-quality options at reasonable prices, or even negotiating for better terms. Luxury doesn't have to be a splurge; it can be a calculated investment that gives you tangible and intangible benefits.

Moreover, smart luxury is not static. As you grow personally and professionally, your priorities and preferences may change. What you once considered a luxury may become less important, while other things may gain relevance. For example, in your early years, you may enjoy investing in entertainment experiences, but later in life you may prefer luxuries related to peace of mind, free time, or your children's education. The key is to adapt to your circumstances and use luxury to enhance your life at each stage.

Smart luxury also has an impact on how others perceive you. A person who knows how to handle luxury with balance and good taste commands respect and admiration. In contrast, someone who is overly ostentatious or spends recklessly can project an image of superficiality or lack of judgment. Luxury should be a tool that reinforces your image, not something that dominates it. When you use it with moderation and purpose, you send a clear message that you have control over your life and your decisions.

Finally, it is important to remember that smart luxury is not an end in itself, but a means to achieve something bigger. It can be a way to reward yourself for your efforts, to inspire you to keep going, to strengthen your relationships or to position yourself better in your environment. When you use luxury consciously, you not only enjoy its benefits, but you also avoid falling into the traps of empty consumption and unnecessary debt.

In short, luxury intelligence is about seeing luxury as a strategic tool that can enhance your life, your position, and your reputation when used purposefully and in moderation. It's not about accumulating expensive things, but about making careful choices that reflect your values, your goals, and your identity. When you learn to master the art of intelligent luxury, you not only improve your quality of life, but you also become an example of success and good judgment for those around you.

The Winners Circle

The people you surround yourself with have a direct impact on your life, your decisions, and ultimately, your success. The winner's circle is that select group of individuals who not only share your ambitions, but also inspire you, challenge you, and push you to reach new heights. Building this circle doesn't just happen; it requires strategy, intention, and above all, a consistent commitment to your own growth.

A winners circle is not about quantity, but about quality. You don't need to surround yourself with hundreds of people, but with a few who really add value to your life. These are people who think big, who aren't afraid to take calculated risks, and who understand the importance of effort, discipline, and vision. They can be entrepreneurs, leaders, experts in their field, or simply people with an exceptional mindset. The important thing is that they are aligned with your goals and share a life philosophy based on growth and progress.

The first step to building a winner's circle is to assess your current environment. Honestly ask yourself if the people you spend the most time with are helping you move forward or, on the contrary, holding you back. This doesn't mean you should cut ties with everyone who doesn't meet this standard, but it does mean being more selective about who you allow to influence your decisions and your way of thinking. People who are negative, complacent, or always find excuses not to move forward can be a burden that you need to let go of.

Once you identify the people you want to surround yourself with, the next step is to create opportunities to connect with them. This can involve attending events, joining professional groups, or simply seeking out mentors and colleagues who inspire you. Networking, when done genuinely, is not just an exchange of business cards, but a way to build relationships based on shared interests and values. It's important to approach these people with an attitude of collaboration and learning, not just thinking about what you can get out of it, but what you can contribute.

A winners circle isn't static; it evolves with you. As you grow and reach new goals, your needs and priorities change, and so do the people in your life. Some relationships may strengthen, while others may naturally fade away. This isn't a negative thing, but rather a sign that you're moving forward. Don't be afraid to reevaluate your circle from time to time to make sure it's still a reflection of your current goals and aspirations.

The key to maintaining a winner's circle is reciprocity. You can't expect to surround yourself with successful and motivating people if you're not willing to be one of them too. This means constantly working on yourself, improving your skills, maintaining a positive attitude, and adding value to the lives of others. A winner's circle is not formed from selfishness or unfair competition, but from collaboration and mutual support. When you help others succeed, you create an environment where everyone can thrive.

Another crucial aspect of a winner's circle is honesty. These are the people who aren't afraid to tell you the truth, even when it's not what you want to hear. A true winner won't surround you with empty praise or feed your illusions. Instead, they'll offer you constructive criticism and challenge you to be better. This type of feedback may be uncomfortable, but it's essential to your growth. Learn to value and seek out these types of relationships, because they're the ones that will truly help you move forward.

It's important to understand that a winner's circle isn't limited to your professional life. It also includes people who support you emotionally, believe in you, and remind you of your values when things get tough. Success isn't just about material or professional achievements; it also involves having balance, personal satisfaction, and a strong support network. The people in your circle should be those who celebrate your successes, but are also there to offer you support and perspective when you face challenges.

Don't forget that you are also responsible for cultivating these relationships. Maintaining a winner's circle takes time, energy, and dedication. This means being present, showing genuine interest in others' goals and challenges, and being willing to invest in these relationships. A winner's circle isn't built overnight, but when you do, its impact on your life is transformative.

Finally, remember that the winners circle is not an exclusive club that only a select few have access to. It is an environment that you create and cultivate with intention. It is not about seeking out the richest or most famous people, but those who truly reflect the values and mindset you want to have. You have the power to attract these people into your life if you work on becoming a winner yourself. When you do, you not only transform your environment, but also your potential for success.

Protect Your Empire

Building an empire, whether financial, professional or personal, is an achievement that requires time, effort and dedication. But the real challenge is not just in achieving it, but in protecting it. What many people don't understand is that success is not a finish line, but a state that must be continually safeguarded and strengthened. Protecting your empire means adopting smart strategies, anticipating risks and making decisions that ensure its long-term stability.

Protecting your empire begins with the understanding that no resource, no matter how abundant, is unlimited. Wealth, time, connections, and energy are valuable assets that must be carefully managed. One of the most common mistakes successful people make is believing that what they have built is indestructible. This overconfidence can lead to carelessness, poor financial decisions, or a lack of foresight in the face of changes in the environment. Protecting your empire requires humility to accept that, no matter how solid it may seem, there are always vulnerabilities.

A key way to protect your empire is to diversify your income. Never rely on just one source of money, even if it seems very stable. Economies change, markets fluctuate, and opportunities that seem surefire today may disappear tomorrow. Investing in different areas, such as real estate, stocks, businesses, and personal projects, gives you a safety net. If one part of your empire faces difficulties, the others can keep it afloat. Diversification is more than a financial strategy; it's a mindset that prepares you for the unexpected.

In addition to diversifying, you need to protect your assets with insurance and legal protections. Many people see insurance as an unnecessary expense, but the truth is that it is an investment in peace of mind. Whether it is health insurance, life insurance, property insurance or even liability insurance, these instruments are designed to protect you and your loved ones from financial blows that can destabilize your empire. Likewise, having a good lawyer and a solid legal plan protects you from potential conflicts or claims that could jeopardize what you have built.

Another key way to protect your empire is to keep your finances organized. This doesn't just mean keeping a tight rein on your income and expenses, but also planning for the future. Having a well-stocked emergency fund is one of the best ways to protect yourself against unexpected events, such as an economic crisis, a health problem, or a business setback. This fund should be large enough to cover at least six months of your basic expenses. When you have this financial cushion, you can face challenges calmly and without making impulsive decisions.

Protecting your empire also means surrounding yourself with the right people. Not all relationships are beneficial to your stability. It's important to identify who is really in your life to support you and who might be there out of convenience or self-interest. Toxic people, unreliable partners, and friendships that drain your energy are threats that can undermine your success from within. A solid circle of loyal, competent people with similar values to yours not only protects you emotionally, but also contributes to strengthening your empire.

Education and continued learning are another essential tool to protect your empire. The world is constantly changing, and what you know today could become obsolete in a few years. Stay up to date with trends in your industry, new technologies, and emerging opportunities. The more informed you are, the more prepared you will be to adapt and make decisions that protect and expand what you have achieved. Investing in your knowledge and skills is one of the best ways to protect your future.

Digital security is an issue that cannot be ignored in today's world. If a significant part of your empire relies on online systems, such as bank accounts, digital businesses, or sensitive information, you need to take steps to protect yourself against potential cyberattacks. This includes using strong passwords, two-factor authentication, backup systems, and working with cybersecurity experts when necessary. A lapse in this area can cost you dearly and jeopardize what you spent years building.

It's also important to think about the legacy of your empire. If something were to happen to you, what would happen to everything you've built? Preparing a will, setting up trusts, or structuring an estate plan not only protects your family, but also ensures that your legacy continues. Many people avoid these types of conversations because they seem distant or uncomfortable, but leaving these topics unresolved can lead to conflict and loss that could have easily been avoided.

Finally, protecting your empire also means protecting yourself. Your physical, mental, and emotional health is the foundation of everything you build. Without it, even the strongest empire can crumble. Prioritize rest, exercise, good nutrition, and stress-reducing practices. Also, surround yourself with people and activities that energize and motivate you. Your well-being is not a luxury, it is a necessity to maintain the balance and strength required to run your empire.

Protecting your empire is not an act of paranoia, but of wisdom. It is understanding that success is not guaranteed and that every step you take must be backed by careful planning and a proactive attitude. What you have built is valuable, and taking care of it is not only a sign of gratitude for what you have achieved, but also a way to ensure that you can enjoy its fruits for a long time to come. A protected empire is an empire that can grow, endure, and transcend, becoming a legacy that goes beyond your own lifetime.

How to be Remembered as a Winner

Being remembered as a winner has less to do with how much money you made or how many accomplishments you achieved, but rather the impact your life had on others. People who leave a lasting mark on the world understand that true success is not just measured in numbers, but in how they inspire, help and uplift those around them. A winner is not just someone who made it to the top, but someone who leveraged that position to build a legacy that transcends their time.

To be remembered as a winner, the first thing you must do is live according to your deepest values. People don't remember the details of each of your decisions, but they will always remember how you made them feel. If your life is guided by integrity, respect, and authenticity, you will leave an indelible impression. This means being consistent with your actions, not only in moments of success, but also in challenges. Sticking to your principles, even when it's hard, is what truly defines your character.

The next step is to positively impact the lives of others. Winners don't focus solely on themselves; they understand that their success can be a vehicle for improving the world. This doesn't mean you have to donate millions of dollars or found an organization, although that can be part of your legacy, too. It can be as simple as inspiring others by your example, offering your time as a mentor, or sharing your knowledge to help someone move forward on their own path. The important thing is that every interaction you have is an opportunity to leave something positive behind.

Another crucial aspect is the ability to lead with humility. A true winner doesn't need to boast about his or her achievements or put others down to feel important. Humility allows you to connect with people in a genuine and meaningful way. When you are seen as someone who acknowledges your own mistakes, celebrates the successes of others, and never forgets where you come from, you become an admirable and respected figure. Being humble doesn't mean minimizing your achievements, but rather using them as a tool to inspire and motivate others.

Leaving a lasting legacy also means building something that will outlive your time. This can be a business, a social project, an idea, or even a family tradition that transcends generations. The important thing is that what you create has a clear purpose and a tangible impact. For example, if you are an entrepreneur, think about how your business can contribute to the well-being of your employees and the community. If you are a creator, focus on producing something that inspires or educates. If you build with the intention of leaving something that benefits others, your influence will remain even when you are gone.

The way you handle moments of adversity also defines how you will be remembered. Everyone faces obstacles, but the winners are those who face them with courage, determination and a resilient attitude. Showing strength in the midst of difficulty inspires others and shows that success is not just a matter of talent, but of perseverance. People remember those who, despite their falls, got up stronger and learned from their failures. These stories are the ones that have the most impact and remain in the collective memory.

Your relationship with time is another important factor. A winner knows that time is their most valuable resource and uses it wisely. This doesn't just mean being productive, but also making sure your time is spent on what really matters. Spend time with loved ones, cultivate meaningful relationships, and make space for your passions. No one wants to be remembered as someone who was too busy to live. When you prioritize what has value, you create memories that stay in people's hearts.

Another fundamental point is how you choose to treat those who are in less privileged positions than you. A genuine winner does not use his or her power or success to oppress, but to empower. Treating everyone with dignity, regardless of their status or condition, demonstrates a level of greatness that transcends material achievements. The way you make others feel, especially those who have less than you, is one of the things that is most remembered about a person.

Lastly, to be remembered as a winner, you must live an authentic life. This means being true to yourself and not trying to fit into a mold that others have defined for you. Authenticity has a magnetic power; when you live according to who you truly are, you inspire others to do the same. People don't connect with perfection, they connect with humanity. Share your struggles, your learnings, and your dreams. An authentic life is a life that is remembered because it is full of meaning.

Being remembered as a winner doesn't happen by accident. It's the result of conscious choices, living with purpose, and understanding that true success is found in the impact you leave on the world. Build something that matters, treat others with respect and kindness, and live each day as an opportunity to contribute. When you do, you won't just be remembered as someone who was successful, but as someone who made a real difference and left a legacy that will last beyond time.

Your Money, Your Eternal Voice

Money, when used with wisdom and purpose, can become a voice that transcends your time and space. It is a tool that not only reflects who you are, but also how you choose to impact the world. While words can be forgotten and individual acts can fade over time, the strategic actions you take with your money have the power to resonate for generations. Your money, well managed, becomes an echo of your values, your priorities, and your vision for the future.

Thinking of your money as your eternal voice means using it in a way that represents what you truly care about. It's not just about accumulating wealth for the pleasure of having it, but investing it in projects, causes, and people that reflect your beliefs and goals. Every decision you make with your money sends a message, not just to the people around you, but to the world at large. When you choose to spend on something, support a cause, or build a business, you're defining the narrative of who you are and what you stand for.

One of the most powerful ways to make your voice eternal is through strategic investments. When you invest in assets that generate wealth over the long term, you are ensuring that your impact is not ephemeral. Whether you choose to focus on real estate, businesses, or financial markets, the important thing is that your money works for you and continues to produce even when you are gone. This steady stream of income not only benefits you, but also gives you the opportunity to extend your influence over time.

Another key way to use your money as your eternal voice is to support causes that align with your values. Think about the social or environmental issues that matter most to you. Maybe you care about education, access to healthcare, environmental protection, or empowering marginalized communities. By funding projects that seek to solve these problems, you are creating an impact that will last beyond your lifetime. The people you help, directly or indirectly, will always remember your contribution, even if they never get to meet you in person.

Your money can also be a tool to educate and inspire future generations. Consider creating educational scholarships, donating books, funding workshops, or even establishing an investment fund that your children and grandchildren can use to build their own dreams. When you use your wealth to open doors for others, you are leaving a tangible legacy that not only changes lives, but also perpetuates your vision of success as something bigger than yourself.

Plus, building a purpose-driven business is a great way to make your voice stick. Entrepreneurs who create companies with a positive impact on society are building more than just a revenue stream; they are building institutions that reflect their worldview. A well-designed business can continue to operate and benefit society long after you retire. For example, if you build a company that fosters sustainability or promotes innovation, your money will be working to improve the world for decades.

Being generous with your time and resources can also strengthen the impact of your voice. Philanthropy isn't just for billionaires. No matter how much you have, you can always find a way to contribute. Maybe it's donating to a cause close to your heart, supporting a family in your community, or even funding small projects that make a meaningful impact. These actions speak to who you are and leave a positive memory in those who benefit from your generosity.

To make your money truly your eternal voice, you need to plan ahead. This involves creating a will, setting up trusts, and organizing your estate in a way that reflects your wishes and goals. It's not just about avoiding conflicts between heirs, but about making sure your assets continue to be used in a way that represents your values. A solid, well-structured financial plan is an essential tool to ensure your legacy remains intact.

Discipline also plays a crucial role in this equation. Using your money as an eternal voice requires making conscious decisions and avoiding impulsive or unnecessary spending. It's not that you should deprive yourself of enjoying what you've earned, but you do need to balance the present with the future. Every expense should be an investment, whether it's in experiences, personal growth, or something that will provide long-term value. This mindset ensures that your wealth doesn't disperse, but rather multiplies and lasts.

Finally, using your money as your eternal voice means leaving an emotional mark. Beyond numbers and material goods, what really lasts is how you made people feel. Maybe you paid for someone's education, helped a family in a critical moment, or inspired others with your success story. These actions, although sometimes seem small, are the ones that truly remain in the memory of those who experience them. Your money is not just a resource, it is a tool to amplify your humanity.

When you start to see your money as an extension of your purpose and not just a means to meet your immediate needs, you begin to build a voice that will resonate far beyond your time. It's a reminder that the true power of money isn't in how much you have, but in what you choose to do with it. Your legacy won't just be a reflection of your wealth, but of your ability to use it in a way that inspires, transforms, and leaves the world a little better than you found it.

www.ingramcontent.com/pod-product-compliance
Lightning Source LLC
LaVergne TN
LVHW090422210926
848480LV00002B/655
9798227523662